ZEN FABLES FOR TODAY

ZEN FABLES FOR TODAY

STORIES INSPIRED BY THE ZEN MASTERS

RICHARD McLEAN

AVON BOOKS  NEW YORK

AVON BOOKS
A division of
The Hearst Corporation
1350 Avenue of the Americas
New York, New York 10019

Copyright © 1998 by Richard McLean
Front cover illustration by Maggie Oster
Inside back cover author photograph by Richard McLean
Text design by Stanley S. Drate/Folio Graphics Co. Inc.
Published by arrangement with the author
Visit our webside at **http://www.AvonBooks.com**
ISBN: 0-380-79561-2

Library of Congress Cataloging in Publication Data:

McLean, Richard.
    Zen fables for today : stories inspired by the Zen masters /
  Richard McLean.
      p. cm.
    Includes index.
    1. Zen Buddhism—Anecdotes. I. Title.
  BQ9266.M39 1998   97-45494
  294.3'927—dc21   CIP

First Avon Books Trade Printing: March 1998

AVON TRADEMARK REG. U.S. PAT. OFF. AND IN OTHER COUNTRIES, MARCA
REGISTRADA, HECHO EN U.S.A.

Printed in the U.S.A.

OPM 10 9 8 7 6 5 4 3 2 1

For my sweet Marcia

Contents

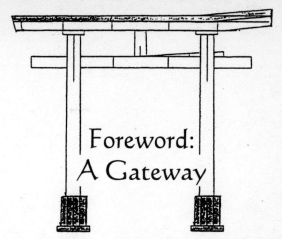

Foreword: A Gateway

When first I read the classic Zen fables, I was struck by the wisdom wrapped up in these deceptively simple parables. Though many lessons were set in other times and other cultures, I found that their truths speak to us today.

In this telling, old fables are re-created and new fables developed from the rich melody of Zen philosophy. They sing of old times as well as the present, but all sing of the human condition, which never changes.

I make no claims to profound knowledge of Buddhism nor startling insights that are not found elsewhere—and better stated at that! Rather than trying to articulate the profound lyrics of Zen Buddhism, I have sought to hum the music.

These stories can be read slowly; picked up and put down as suits the reader's taste.

The simplified descriptions of Zen principles are contained in a section of their own as is a list of Gateway Reading at the end of the book.

I should like to present this book as a work that points to the gateway rather than presumes to be the guide. I have described Zen Buddhism from my limited understanding in the hopes that if the reader is interested, the reader can venture ahead in far more expert company.

ZEN PRIMER

For those interested in the principles underlying
Buddhism, this section may prove informative.
It strives to simplify rather than complicate at the
risk of only skimming the surface. But even at its
surface Buddhism and its child, Zen Buddhism,
offer new ways of viewing old problems with
solutions that have enriched participants
for over twenty centuries.
As noted in the Foreword, the author claims no
profound knowledge but rather a sense of
awe—somewhat like the gatekeeper who only
points the way to the temple.

Zen Buddhism

Zen is impossible to approach from a purely logical standpoint. Zen pays limited homage to the intellectual and insists that to understand the metaphysical universe one must rely upon intuition and experience to break the old patterns of thought and come to stunning insights.

Zen warns about the "trap of words" that substitute intellectualization for true insights. Thus, for the beginner Zen seems filled with paradoxes and contradictions. However, with time these problems become less troublesome.

The noted scholar Huston Smith summarizes the condition of life that Zen seeks to obtain as follows:

- The condition in which life and the awareness that forms its core are experienced as distinctly good.
- With the perception of life's goodness comes an outlook that others are as important as we are.
- The life of Zen does not draw the individual away from the world but returns the individual with a new perspective (and responsibility).
- With this perspective of the infinite there comes an attitude of agreeable acceptance of life in its totality.
- As the concept of oneness grows, the separateness of self and others, finite and infinite, life and death are transcended until ultimately the individual finds singular joy in today without fear of a tomorrow.

Zen is not otherworldly. Zen is compassionate. Zen addresses the problem of today as aptly as did the Buddha 2,500 years ago.

Buddha, the Man

Buddha stands as a unique personality among the founders of other great systems of metaphysical thought. He refused to accept the adoration of the masses. In a famous interchange he was asked:

> *"Are you a god?"*
> *"No."*
> *"Are you an angel?"*
> *"No."*
> *"Are you a prophet?"*
> *"No."*
> *"Then what are you?"*
> *"I am one who is awake."*

He eschewed the trappings of religion and forbade ritual and religious structure. Buddha's focus was upon the here and now and pragmatic ways to live a richer, fuller life.

Two of his key teachings:

1. The conviction that each person must find his or her own answers, that all learning is only a tool. And these essential answers must come from the person's experience both internal and external. Buddha asked of his followers great faith, great doubt, and great effort.

   "Be a lamp unto yourself."

2. Enormous sense of compassion for life and all living things. Tough-minded and a strict teacher, his essential characteristic was one of love.

When a friend accidentally served him a poisoned meal, one of his dying acts was to assure the disconsolate disciple that it was "okay," that the meal had been one of the two best meals of his life—the meal that fueled his body when he achieved enlightenment and the meal that ended this last incarnation.

Since his words are as fresh today as when they were first uttered 2,500 years ago we know that they have universal wisdom and relevance to today and today's problems.

Enlightenment

Satori, or enlightenment, is one of the goals of Zen Buddhism. In much of Zen literature it is described as a sudden and dramatic awakening to the central concepts of the universe and our place in that universe. It mirrors the quest of the original Buddha, who stubbornly sat beneath the bodhi tree until he reached his state of enlightenment.

In much (too much, in some opinions) of Zen literature enlightenment is the climax of a drama wherein an individual meditates and studies and wrestles with Koans (riddles) until some nonrelated event triggers this shattering religious experience that leaves the individual changed forever and initiates the person in the first step in Zen development.

This kind of enlightenment is fine, but there are also gradual awakenings, little bursts of insight that in the aggregate form a new vision of reality and the universe. Whether there's a sudden or a gradual awakening, the result may be similar.

Compassion

Of all the aspects of Buddhism, compassion is one of its sweetest virtues. For a supposedly abstract philosophy it holds human and all life in profound reverence. Buddhism teaches that we are literally all one—humanity, nature, and animals—all part of an integrated whole. Flowing from this concept is the dictum that we show compassion just as compassion is given us in the magnificent "suchness of things." If she had a voice, Buddhism would shout at us, "Take care of your little sister!"

Nonduality

Nonduality is a complicated concept that offers the suggestion that our Western thinking is far too black and white. Buddhism says that there is no difference between:

> self and others
> man and nature
> intellect and intuition
> good and evil
> life and death

Buddhism sees each thing as an indivisible part of a magnificent whole.

Even the hint of truth in this concept opens wondrous new ways of thinking:

- If self and others are one, then we must treat others as we would like to be treated (sound familiar?).
- If man and nature are one, then we must not be profligate in our use of the earth's resources, both animal and material.
- If intellect and intuition are one, then we in the West must open ourselves to new doors of thought and learning.
- If good and evil are one, then maybe we should see the good in some evils and the evil in some saintly actions.

- If life and death are only different phases of the same reality, then the intimation of death becomes less burdensome.

By opening the mind to the concept of nonduality, we become less judgmental and more open to the world. Most important we become more open to ourselves.

Mindfulness

The Zen concept of mindfulness could be described as "time hedonism." Zen offers a view of the world that is starkly practical; it says we can (and must) live in the present. And the only way to live in the present is to be present in the moment. For example, if we are washing dishes, Zen says to be there washing the dishes and living that simple action rather than tuning out.

Zen labels as wasteful recriminations over the past or worry about the future. "Live now," it commands and gives us the tool to live now: mindfulness of the moment, living in the present, not squandering this precious span of life, not putting consciousness on "automatic pilot" or dreaming away today in favor of an impossible-to-predict tomorrow.

Karma

The belief in Karma stems from older beliefs in reincarnation—that in succeeding lives we will still carry with us the good and the bad from previous lives. And perhaps by good actions in this life we may avoid having to pay for them in future incarnations. Some hold that what we do unto others will in turn be done to us in a future life.

Also within the concept of Karma is the acceptance that much of what we are has come from a previous life and yet we have the power to overcome those negative aspects of self and grow in wisdom and love.

A sense of Karma urges us to act, to overcome old habits, and to accept responsibility for ourselves today despite the past.

Nonviolence

Nonviolence is another treasure from Buddhist belief. From its reverence for life and its dictum of compassion, war (and other forms of violence) are eschewed. Sweetly lacking in Buddhist history is a history of "holy wars."

This precept of nonviolence lives as a personal doctrine that teaches that the true nonviolence begins within the self and radiates outward to the world. The opposition to war by Buddhist groups the world over shines as a golden thread in the fabric of this gentle garment of wisdom.

Meditation

Meditation plays an important role in Zen Buddhism. This practice is based on a dazzling view of the human as having the capacity to find one's own way to the truth for one's self from one's innate wisdom. The art (and the trick) is to strip off all the layers of ignorance, ego, and conditioning that make it difficult to reach the core self.

The techniques developed over years of experience are available in many Zen and non-Zen texts as well as practice sessions for beginners in Zen communities. The physical and mental health benefits of meditation have been touted for years, but like all things worthwhile, meditation takes work.

In the Gateway Reading section (a short list of entrance books for those with a beginning curiosity about Zen) you will find a fine book on meditation by a medical doctor, Herbert Benson, who has no Buddhist background to my knowledge.

If you take nothing else from your interest in Zen than a capacity to meditate, you will come away enriched for a lifetime.

Kitchen Zen

says nine things about meditation:

I Don't break your hips trying to sit the way the Orientals do because your Occidental body is different. Be centered with a back stiff enough to keep you alert and not falling asleep. If necessary sit in a chair or even lie flat.

2 Start by counting the breaths up to ten and then start over. Sounds easy; it's hard as hell. But do it and do it and do it until you feel your counting slowing.

3 As a visual, imagine your belly button is your nose; breathe in to fill the belly, then imagine breathing out through your ears.

4 Put a chimney in the very top of your head. Let extraneous thoughts, worries, erotic images, and the like pass out through the chimney (not unlike gas). Then return to your breathing.

5 Calm the "chattering monkey of the mind." Unthinking may be the most difficult mental exercise you've ever tried. Sit with half-closed, unfocused eyes.

❧

6 Keep in mind that meditation in the Western context means "to think hard upon an issue"; meditation in the Zen context means the opposite.

❧

7 What you find in meditation will often scare the hell out of you. Push on bravely. Trust that you will come out the other end of the smoky tunnel.

❧

8 Do it regularly, not necessarily religiously. Start with just five minutes. Keep expectations modest. If you give up, come back to it.

❧

9 After your twenty-five to fifty minutes of meditation ends, take time for introspection. Review what you discarded and what you found: discards are valuable lessons in what is eating at you, and discoveries provide nourishment from your own intrinsic wisdom.

Humor

Humor ranks as one of Zen's most delightful characteristics. Humor pricks the balloon of pretension; humor illuminates with laughter subtle truths lost in preaching. Humor—like Zen—emerges deep from within the self. Just as no one can make us laugh, so too no one can make us see the truth about ourselves or the world.

Do not be fooled by the often frivolous form of these fables. They come in jest but they come with a mission (kind of like the way your mother slipped the medicine in your orange juice).

The Ordinary

As opposed to cathedrals and evangelical expressions, Zen takes its strength from the splendidly ordinary. Like the Zen art of haiku poetry or brush painting, the Zen experience celebrates simple and sparse expression. Zen warns that an enlightened person "does not display this enlightenment like a piece of dog droppings on the end of the nose." It brings the wonders of Zen discovery into ordinary life. The sheer ritual of going about one's life becomes meaningful and joyous. One Western student who had been in training in Japan for seven years described it this way, "No parapsychic experiences, as far as I am aware. But you wake up in the morning and the world seems so beautiful you can hardly believe it."

Visualizing Buddhism as an Elegant Buffet

One of the marvels of Buddhism is that interested parties don't have to make a religious commitment. It can be used as a relevant ethical system or a functional self-help device or provide new ways to cope with our complex society. Or Buddhism can become a nourishing spiritual path. At all levels this multitiered system proves enriching.

Imagine Buddhism as an elegant buffet with these choices:

Just cruising the dessert tray

Enjoy the amusing anecdotes as well as chomping on the rich nuggets of wisdom. Leaves a lingering sweet taste.

Digging into the salad bar

Discover pragmatic solutions to everyday problems. Find old ideas that are as fresh as tomatoes picked in the field that morning.

Pigging out on favorite pastas

Put into use tested techniques for modifying consciousness and behavior. Have adventures as exciting as finding a new Italian restaurant.

Filling up on brain food

Find insights into different systems of philosophy and thought. Discover that Eastern thought is as different from Western thought as seafood is from meat.

Dining on heavy-duty meats

Tackle new ways of dealing with profound questions such as: Who am I? What is my place in the universe? And how do I reconcile with my own mortality? Protein stuff!

Buying a meal ticket and becoming a regular

Buddhism may open a new journey into spirituality. No, it isn't necessary to shave the head and find a begging bowl. Buddhism is as much a religion of the world as a religion of the monastery. Ask the millions of practitioners!

I

A morning glory.
And so, today, may seem,
My own story.

II

A butterfly
Asleep, perched upon
The temple bell.

III

A thief
Left it behind . . .
the moon at the window

Portrait of Bashō (1644–1694) One of the sweetest singers Japan has ever given the world, this haiku genius defined the unique seventeen-syllable verse form. Like the koans and minimalist art of Zen, one does better to feel the work rather than try to "solve" it rationally. *Artist:* Hokusai (1873).

THE FABLES

"Like honey in the mouth of a mute"
is what a sense of Zen should be—according to
the Zen Masters—because Zen can never be
captured in words or pictures. And like the
honey in the mouth of the mute, Zen should
be a private joy. The metaphor warns people
new to Zen to resist the impulse to
"teach the world to Zen."
Unlike the mute, who savors a glorious
sweetness and can not describe it, this author
must speak, however imperfectly;
hence this small book.

A failed monk named Ichhi labored his whole life in the kitchen of the great monastery at Lake Hakkone. He was deemed a "failed monk" by himself and his superiors because he had been assigned the koan of "What is the sound of one hand clapping?" since his earliest days in the congregation and had never been able to solve it. It was now fifty-five years of failure and he was nearing the end of his lifetime.

But as he lay dying he suddenly realized that he cradled a great peace in his soul. Gone was the striving for enlightenment, gone was the stridency of his loins, and gone was the haunting koan—for he had found the stillness of no longer striving in this exquisite silence alone in the attic in the soft dark at the end of his life.

It was only then, when there remained no more questions nor need for answers (or even the need for breathing) that Ichhi heard at last the whooshing silence of one hand clapping.

While the house slept,

the mother slipped out of her bed, into her robe, and down to the kitchen to make her children's lunches.

As she wrote the name on each of the bags, she held that special offspring in her mind.

She laid out the bread yet refused to produce sandwiches assembly-line style. The mother made one lunch at a time, being one with the doing, while imagining the child eating the lunch.

Peanut butter with grape jelly on brown bread for her youngest. The apple peeled because the new braces hurt her teeth and two chocolate chip cookies, one for recess time. She included a dinner-size napkin because her last-born was a spiller. She smiled as she folded up the brown sack and placed a quarter for milk beside it.

She smiled also as she started the next lunch.

With the awaking one by one of her family, she followed the happy noise that began upstairs then worked its way down to the kitchen for breakfast, then into the hall, out the door, and toward the bus stop.

"Did you kiss them goodbye?" asked her husband.

"I kissed them," said the mother watching her precious cargo with their lunches board the school bus.

> ❧ *Here lies a beautiful example of how a simple morning routine—when carried out mindfully—becomes a ritual of love that enriches both the giver and the receivers.*

Jato, the instructor to the Emperor's sons, observed that the oldest boy was given to outbursts of anger, which could prove dangerous in later life because this prince stood as heir to his aging father's throne and armies. One day in the midst of the boy's tantrum, Jato dragged the youth to a flowering bush and thrust the prince's hand against a cluster of feeding bees until one bee stung the boy.

The prince was so surprised that anyone would treat him so roughly that he stopped his raging. Cradling his stinging hand he yelled at Jato, "I am going to tell my father."

"When you tell your father, tell him this . . ."

"What?"

"Look at the bee."

Together they studied the bee writhing on a leaf with its entrails torn out with the stinger. They watched the agonized insect until it died.

"That is the price of anger," said Jato.

That night the boy told his father, who gave Jato a gold piece. The boy, when he became emperor, was known for his quiet judgment and his unwillingness to be provoked. This latter trait proved invaluable during his long reign through turbulent times.

"Lord Buddha can take me whenever he wants," said the patroness of the temple. "I am old; I have lived a full life."

Each evening she would visit the temple, light incense, and intone these words for all to hear.

One night two boys hid behind the statue of the Buddha and boomed out:

"Prepare, old woman. Tonight is the night."

With which the old woman died of fright.

Although the two boys never told anyone of their deed, they carried with them for the rest of their lives an immense respect for words and the power locked inside a simple sentence or a mindless jest.

"Oh boy! Oh boy!" cried the monk-on-probation who had just cracked the Zen Master's favorite (and valuable) drinking cup.

The frightened youngster went to the Zen Master and asked, "Why must there be death?"

The Master answered, "Death is natural. It comes to all persons and things. We should not greet it with fear or meet death with anger. Why do you ask?"

"Because, Master, death has come upon your cup."

A Zen master and one of his best students were returning late at night to a mountain monastery when a brutal winter storm caught them on the treacherous path. To stop meant dying of exposure; to go on meant the risk of falling to certain death from the slippery cliffs.

The only method of navigating was offered by the flashes of lightning that would illuminate the trail ahead. Slowly, amid the banshee winds and biting rain, the pair crept forward.

When they feared they had lost their way, they would wait for the lightning and memorize the trail ahead with the lingering image left behind their eyes.

At last they reached the monastery. While drying off and eating a late supper in the kitchen, the student confessed to the teacher that what he feared most was that he would die without attaining enlightenment.

"Enlightenment," confessed the teacher, "is not the sun that shines all day but the lightning that gives only quick glimpses—thus allowing us to navigate from one troubled place to another."

"Is that true for you, Master?" asked the student.

"It's true for most of us," whispered the master.

Enlightenment is not unique to Zen. It happens to all of us in little doses at different times in those stunning personal insights about our place in the universe. These mini-enlightenments come (like lightning) then fade and are augmented by other insights that help light our paths.

An aged monk, who had lived a long and active life, was assigned a chaplain's role at an academy for girls. In discussion groups he often found that the subject of love became a central topic.

This comprised his warning to the young women:

"Understand the danger of anything-too-much in your lives. Too much anger in combat can lead to recklessness and death. Too much ardor in religious beliefs can lead to close-mindedness and persecution. Too much passion in love creates dream images of the beloved—images that ultimately prove false and generate anger.

"To love too much is to lick the honey from the point of the knife."

"But as a celibate monk," asked one young woman, "how can you know of love between a man and a woman?"

"Sometime, dear children," replied the old teacher, "I will tell you why I became a monk."

"I'm angry with you," said one sister to the other sister as both returned from their mother's funeral.

"Why?"

"Because you didn't act appropriately at the funeral."

"What do you mean?" replied her sister.

"You seemed to be having too much of a good time."

"I was."

"How can you say that with your mother dead only five days?"

"I think sorrow and joy run on parallel paths like two horses pulling the same wagon. The important thing is to recognize each in its place and in its time."

"But you were laughing and . . ."

"Sure, I found joy in seeing old friends. I loved talking about Mother and reliving happy memories. The grieving I do on my own. If I seemed happy, I was—in that moment. And I liked the food."

"But what about appearances?"

"Appearances are your problem not mine."

"You are right about the food, though."

"I'm right about the joy, too."

The unmarried daughter of the woodcutter hid in the tall closet with her young son as she heard the soldiers pillaging and killing. She could trace their progress down her street by the screams.

This street marked the boundaries of her world. Here she fed birds in the winter and raised her son, born out of wedlock not from the hunger of her flesh but the aching need of her betrothed, now run away. Here she had cared for her father until his death and then, as if out of habit, she cared for neighbors. "Get the woodcutter's daughter," they would advise, and she would come. Loving and beloved, she planned to die on this street, but not this day, not with her precious son.

She knew a soldier had come to her yard because her brave dog barked a furious bark until it ceased in a mid-bark yelp. Then she heard someone ransacking the house and whispered to her little boy, "We're playing hide and seek. Don't make a sound."

The lone soldier, drunk with killing, ripped open the tall closet door. The woodcutter's daughter covered her son's eyes then stripped open her bath kimono. The shock of her nakedness cause the warrior to lower his sword as his eyes licked down her soft body.

In that instant, the woodcutter's daughter swung her kindling hatchet in a pure arc cleaving the soldier's skull, and he plummeted downward following the hatchet's arc like a low bow to death.

"Fall down, go boom" explained the mother to her son

as she uncovered his eyes. Then stepping over the corpse she made her escape into the night.

🖎 *Zen teaching—like life itself—recognizes that we must often choose between the lesser of two evils. Here the principles of nonviolence balance between self-defense and submitting to the violence of the marauding soldier.*

The bewitched moth

flew in ever-tighter circles around and around the pure but deadly flame of the candle.

Seeing the moth's fatal trajectory the fly shouted, "Beware, my foolish friend. To continue your course means certain death."

"Well," replied the moth to the fly, "when *you* can give up your addiction to that smelly manure, *then* you may presume to lecture me."

"But you will die for sure, friend Moth."

"How could anything so beautiful . . . anything that feels so exquisite be harmful?" asked the moth.

"Have you ever been in love?" asked the fly.

"No."

"Then you could never understand," said the fly as he sadly watched his friend flutter in closing circles until at last with a "phsst" the flame ate him.

✍ *Those of us who have been wildly in love understand this parable completely. Those who have loved more coolly could never understand.*

Two panicky city dwellers found themselves lost in the high timber. After wandering for a day and a night, they came upon an old hermit.

"How do we find our way back to civilization?" they asked the hermit.

"I could tell you but you'd still get lost," replied the hermit.

"What should we do?" they asked.

"Go with the flow."

"I beg your pardon?"

"Go with the flow. You see that stream over there. Just follow it. Streams go into creeks and creeks go into rivers and rivers go through towns. Also, along the way you'll have water to drink and berries to eat."

"Is that what Zen people mean when they say 'go with the flow'?"

"Yes and no," replied the hermit proceeding along his way.

🍂 *"Go with the flow" is an expression that emanates from Zen practice. Like the water in the stream we are advised to accept what life gives us as it takes us to our ultimate ocean.*

A clever ruler, known for his guile, maintained balance in his kingdom by pitting his two most skillful generals against each other. The ruler's spies whispered lies to keep the commanders in constant agitation (so that they would not combine in revolt against the ruler).

"See how your rival's cavalry attacks with such precision? Why can't *your* cavalry do as well?" he would ask one.

And then say to the other, "Send your infantry to take lessons from the other general."

In battle each general vied to outdo the other. To add zest to a campaign, the ruler would invite each to capture the same city with prizes and praise to the winner and disgrace to the "loser" despite the overall victory.

Needless to say, these generals' hate for each other knew no limits other than the loyalty sworn to their master.

One day the ruler strayed too close to the battle lines and became surrounded by enemy troops intoxicated with the idea of slicing him to ribbons and wearing him on their regimental flags. At the last second, however, a rescue battalion led by one of the generals saved the ruler from certain slaughter.

"Name your prize!" exclaimed the breathless ruler. "Anything within my power."

"Anything?" asked the general with an evil gleam—a look that warned the ruler that the general might ask for his rival's head.

"Yes, anything. However, I must warn you that whatever I give to you, I will give twofold to your brother general."

"Fine!" replied the rescuer, "blind me in one eye."

🖎 *Many who have lived or observed a divorce will find this fable not so far-fetched.*

The aged ailing woman complained to her best friend, "I hate being old. I hate being here in this rest home."

"Let's be positive," began the friend.

"Positive about what? Damn it."

"Well, are you in pain?"

"No."

"Remember how wonderful you felt when the pain finally went away? Was that pleasurable?"

"Yes."

"Consider that the same pleasure is with you now."

"But it's all so horrible here. The food . . ."

"How was your lunch?" asked the best friend.

"Terrible!"

"Totally terrible? Yet you ate it all."

"It was all I had. I had no choice," said the sick woman.

"What one thing was okay?"

"The whipped cream on top of the fruit salad."

"Fine, start there. Think about the whipped cream."

"This talk is all Pollyanna, so phony optimistic."

"Again, tell me why you ate all your lunch?" asked the best friend.

"Because, damn it, that was all I had."

"That's what I'm trying to say, honey."

> *Zen teaches two precious lessons: (1) accept life as it unfolds, the good parts and the bad; (2) live in the moment, being mindful of the small joys.*

The warty frog and the prize goldfish met one summer afternoon in the temple pool.

"Don't you realize how beautiful I am?" bubbled the goldfish flashing her wispy tail.

The frog made no reply.

"I can understand your silence," gloated the goldfish. "I am not only graceful in my movements but I also enhance the golden rays of the sun."

Again, neither answer nor movement from the frog.

"Say something," demanded the goldfish just as a waiting crane speared the sparkling fish and flew into the sky.

"Bye bye," croaked the frog.

Deep in the night the boy awakened to the smell of smoke. Without dressing or even slipping on his sandals, he explored the wooden dormitory where he slept with forty-eight other boys.

He traced the smoke like a dog, letting his nose guide him. When he touched the door to the stairwell, it felt so hot that he ripped his hand away.

"Wake up," he screamed. "Fire. No time for clothes. Run. No, not that way. This way. Make sure we have everyone."

"Hero," was the description in the newspapers and on the citation from the school.

"Buddha," is what the teacher who taught Zen called him. "A buddha is what you were because that is what the word means: 'the awakened one.' Just imagine what it was like for the original Buddha to awaken under the fig tree and perceive a world on fire with despair. If you think about it, he said what you said:

" 'Wake up. (*Seek enlightenment.*)

" 'Fire! (*Suffering.*)

" 'No time for clothes. (*Give up attachments.*)

" 'Not that way, this way. (*The eight-fold path.*)

" 'Be sure we have everyone.' " (*His teaching to the world.*)

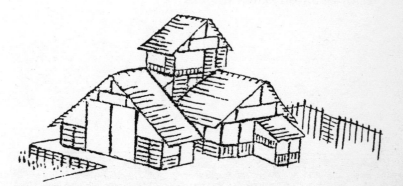

A high-spirited youth attending the Zen archery academy conceived a splendid hoax to confound his classmates. It was the custom that the archers-in-training go out in the early morning and paint circles on various targets and then shoot at them.

The youth slipped out before all the others and fired three arrows at distant objects. Once the arrows hit, he ran out and painted a circle around each, then rushed back to the archery range to await his classmates.

As luck would have it, this was the morning that the master archer chose to visit his students.

"Magnificent," said the master. "Now let us see you do it again."

The boy walked out, retrieved each arrow, and then with classic form skewered each circle again despite the remarkable distances.

"You shall join my advanced class," proclaimed the master.

"How in the world did you pull it off?" whispered the boy's best friend who knew of the hoax.

"It became easy," replied the boy, "once I realized that the arrows already knew the way."

After the desolation of war, the survivors regrouped in what was left of their shattered village. Beyond anguish, the families gathered around their leader, a Zen priest, who said:

"I have no explanations.

"So I will not offer you any. I do not know why you survived and others died. I do not know why this was allowed to happen. I only know that we have our lives and must continue the simple necessities of living.

"To endure is enough.

"Look to the bamboo. The flowers bloom in the spring but die under the heat of summer; yet the bamboo lives all year.

"The summer typhoons blow down the great trees; yet the bamboo bends and in so doing, survives.

"In the freezing of winter when all is brown, the bamboo keeps its jade.

"Look to the bamboo. To endure is enough."

Just before the beginning of time, the goddess Ticca was playing in her garden creating mud figures.

Now it had come to pass that Ticca's mother was so busy scheming with her sisters against her husband's family that  she did not notice that her child had become a young woman capable of creating life. Because of her mother's neglect, Ticca remained unaware of the new powers and responsibilities that womanhood bestowed.

Ticca was so delighted with one exquisitely formed figure that she blew into its nostrils—when it instantly breathed and opened its eyes. Frightened, the young goddess ran to her mother and told her what had happened.

"Naughty, naughty child," scolded the mother. "Did the figure see you when it took life?"

"Just for an instant. Then I disappeared."

"Damn! Well, there's nothing to be done now but tell your father" (who was quite angry because he had to create a whole world to house his daughter's childish folly).

Thus it came to be that Man was created from the innocent affection of one celestial child. However, what Man beheld in that first glimpse has stayed with him through all time: Man's innate sense of his divine origin.

❧ *Buddha's command that we look inward is based on the wondrous conviction that within our DNA—like the legendary glimpse of the mythical Ticca—we all hold a sense of our origins. Zen teaches we need only look, look hard.*

The very important Mr. Tanaka lay in his hospital bed contemplating death. He had already monitored his pulse and written down the results. He had also complained about the meal service and framed a letter suggesting a plan for reorganizing the function.

But now he thought about his dying. He wanted to believe that his business would crumble without him the way his competitor's buildings tumbled down in earthquakes, but he knew the firm would continue and even prosper, as would his wife and children.

"Unless you learn to relax, you will die," said the young doctor. "You are profoundly stressed and the medicines can't really change you, Mr. Tanaka."

The thought of dying terrified Mr. Tanaka, who was always "out of town" for funerals and sent in his stead expensive flowers. He *had* tried to relax. He had tried with all his might, which only sent his blood pressure higher. Now he felt defeated as if his lifelong accomplishments counted for nothing.

"I could die any time," announced Mr. Tanaka.

"Couldn't we all?" agreed his roommate pleasantly.

"I mean *really* die!"

"There's a nonreal death?"

"My name is Mr. Tanaka of Tanaka Construction."

"My name is Professor Suzuki of the Zen middle school."

"What do you teach?"

"Meditation," answered the teacher.

"Perhaps we should talk," said Mr. Tanaka.

🔈 *Zen 101 teaches the splendid cliché, "When the student is ready, the teacher appears."*

The actress looked into the pool and saw a perfect face and perfect teeth and a body that matched.

"Oh, why can't I be a star?" she asked.

"I can make you a star," said the frog.

"Who are you?" exclaimed the actress.

"I am a world-famous producer who has been transformed into a frog by a woman who I hired to play a witch, and who turned out to be a real witch and she cast this spell on me."

"How can I help and what do I get?" asked the actress.

"If you will trade places with me, the spell will be broken and then I will be a world-famous movie producer again and you will appear in all my movies," said the producer-frog.

"Okay," said the actress (who wasn't terribly bright).

"There, it's done. Thank you," said the producer once again returned to his human form.

"But now when do I get to be changed too?" asked the actress-frog.

"Well, honey," said the producer, ". . . that's the catch."

However, true to his word the producer went on to make many successful movies and was known for the quirk of always having a part in his films for a frog.

Be very careful before you wish to trade places with anyone. Your wish might come true!

"The boat is coming to take me home because I have failed in my studies," said the boy to his teacher. "What can I say to my family?"

"Say that you did your best and that is as much as anyone can do," answered the teacher.

"But I wanted to be a famous monk and teach the Sutras."

"You can."

"How?" asked the sad boy.

"Live the sutras. I will show you. Do you see that boat making its way across the lake with the sun setting behind it?"

"Yes."

"Do you see its wake spreading across the lake? See how the boat looks like the apex of a golden triangle as the wake fans out from its bow."

"Sort of . . ."

"Squint," commanded the teacher.

"That boat is you as you leave the monastery. The lake is your life. The wake is the effect that you will have on the world. Each ripple triggers another ripple, which triggers another. By living according to the Precepts, you can teach the Sutras to everyone you meet; a few of these people will pass on your good example to others. Thus the expanding golden wake of good works begets other good works. Most important, notice how each ripple catches the sun and bounces its light back to heaven."

"Would you come home with me and explain all this to my father?"

"This is my cathedral,"

exuded the woman in
the flowery dress while standing amid
the ferns in the grove
of redwood trees.

"Here is where I see God. Here is where I experience nature and man as one. Here I feel a part of the oneness: plants and streams and birds as part of a magnificent whole."

However, when a fly-by bird pooped on her three-hundred-dollar dress, the woman's enthusiasm for birds as a part of the magnificent whole cooled a bit.

"Do I have Buddha mind?"

asked the talking dog.

"Absolutely not," replied Joshu, a famous Zen teacher.

"Why not?" demanded the dog.

"Because you don't reason, you only react."

"Well, who do you think is asking this question?"

"What question?" replied Joshu. "Everyone knows dogs can't talk."

A modern Zen Master, Thich Nhat Hanh*, teaches a beautiful "Hug Meditation," whose recipe is this:

When you hug someone you love, take hold of her and in the first breath, in and out, be totally present with her—noplace else in the world.
Then hold her for three breaths. Nothing more. Nothing less.

It is reported than one man hugged his wife thus in the Atlanta airport on coming home from a retreat, and changed his marriage profoundly thereafter.

> *This meditation cannot be imagined or perceived with the mind. It must be experienced. Try it just once!*

*Thich Nhat Hanh, poet, Zen master, and chairman of the Vietnamese Buddhist Peace Delegation during the Vietnam War, was nominated by Dr. Martin Luther King Jr. for the Nobel Peace Prize. (See Gateway Reading for his simple, yet eloquent works.)

"The miracle worker is coming," shouted the boy monk to his companion. "Come on. We'll see new things and maybe learn more than we could ever learn here."

"You go on," said his young friend. "But tell me all about it when you get back."

When the boy who had gone to see the miracle worker returned, he found his friend sitting in the garden crying. "Why are you crying?" he asked his friend who handed him the poem that he had copied from Lao Tzu:

> There is no need to run outside
> For better seeing.
> Rather abide
> At the center of your being.
>
> For the more you leave it, the less you learn.
> Search your heart and see
> The way to do . . . is to be.

"But tell me why you are crying?" he asked again.

"While you were gone, I had my own small miracle here."

"Where?"

"Here," said the boy, who had stayed behind, pointing at the spot between his eyes.

> ✍ *Small miracles do happen in that awesome silence at the center of one's being whether in meditation or from sudden insights. The miracle worker is you!*

Pride like a pet hawk

perched on the shoulder of the conquering general as he paraded at the head of his army.

"What are *you* doing here?" demanded Pride when he saw Humiliation perched on the other shoulder.

"Where you go, I will go," retorted Humiliation.

But the fortunes of war shifted and soon the general was forced to flee from his shattered army dressed in rags. And by affecting the manners of a beggar, the general was attempting to slip through enemy lines to safety.

"Now do you see how valuable I am?" asked Humiliation.

"Hush," hissed Pride. "Someone will hear you."

"Do you remember me?" asked the woman of the man in the nursing home bed.

"Not exactly," answered the man. "But when you walked in, I felt this warm glow, as if I'd known you for a long time. Maybe it's your sweet smile. Are you new, dear?"

"That's okay, Daddy," said the woman, taking his hand and holding it against her cheek.

 *Imagine that the diminished memory of the sick man is what Karma must be like, like a glimmering from the past or an unexplained impulse.*

A famous teacher took his pupils into a clearing in the forest that was known as a home for wild monkeys. There he took a hollow gourd with a small hole and inserted sweetened rice (a favorite of monkeys). Then he chained the gourd to a stake and waited with his class.

Soon a large monkey approached, sniffed the rice, inserted his paw, and screeched in frustration when he was unable to withdraw his paw (now a fist) through the narrow opening.

Just then a leopard approached and hearing the monkey screeching decided to have monkey for his dinner.

"Let go of the rice. Run!" screamed the pupils, but to no avail because the monkey in his hunger for the rice, refused to let go and was as a consequence caught and eaten by the leopard.

"What was the trap that killed the monkey?" asked the master.

"Rice," said one student.

"The gourd," said another.

"No," replied the wise teacher. "The trap was greed."

A holy monk lived on a vast flood plain, which proved to be a dangerous place during the monsoon season. Despite repeated warnings (and the rising waters) the monk refused to leave his hut.

"In a dream an angel promised me that he would protect me," explained the monk to the many would-be rescuers:

. . . his neighbors who left en masse;

. . . the local officials with a cart;

. . . finally, a rescue team in a boat.

"The angel promised me," he explained loftily.

When the holy monk drowned, the first being he met was the angel of his dreams.

"What are you doing here?" demanded the angel.

"But you promised me . . ." said the monk.

"I kept my promise, you thick-headed old fool! I sent your neighbors, a cart, and a team in a boat."

". . . Oh," replied the monk.

Buddhism is a do-it-yourself kit, not a magic gift. Buddhism asks of its disciples: Great faith, great doubt, and great effort.

"Mama, I'm losing my mind," said the stressed-out young mother.

"You've certainly got your hands full," said her mother.

"Two kids and no child support have got my hands full and my head spinning," said the daughter.

"Honey, I know it's bad, but you'll look back on this as the most fulfilling time of your life."

"Maybe for you and Dad, but not for me."

"You'll see. I only wish that I could have appreciated the wonderful things that happened—while they were happening."

"What wonderful things? Not enough sleep? Not enough money?"

"I've found," said the mother, "that the art of living is to seek in the present all that is wonderful and just put up with the rest."

"Platitudes," mumbled the daughter after the mother—from whom she had wanted to negotiate a loan—had left.

"What's so great about this moment?" she asked, when out of the bedroom clomped a gorgeous, naked three-year-old wearing his sister's rain boots and a helmet made of underpants. The mother whooped and then felt such a stab of love that she skipped from tears of laughter to tears of joy without missing a beat.

Remembering what her mother had said, the young woman wrote a list of all the little joys of the last two days.

And then she started doing the same thing at the end of every day.

Her life stayed the same but her perspective of her life changed and she changed—and only then did her life change.

Her arrest record was worn like a badge of honor by a prominent Buddhist peace activist during the Vietnam War and other antimilitary protests.

However, she retired from the movement explaining: "In protesting for peace I had become as angry and strident as those I was protesting against. One day I found myself holding a placard that said, 'Killing for peace is like screwing for chastity.' And I realized that the paradox was true of me too.

"So I gave up warring for peace in the world and started to work on peace within myself—which is the only place where true peace can begin."

"**Vows of chastity** are serious vows," said the young monk to the older monk.

"I know," said his elder.

"And we make it a solemn practice to avoid the company of women."

"Yes, I know," said the elder. "But what about that young woman over there dressed in her wedding finery who will not be able to attend the ceremony unless someone carries her across the river?"

"We have our rules, which are not to be broken," said the new monk (who knew all the rules by heart).

"But what about the rule of compassion? See? She is crying. Without our help, she will miss her sister's wedding."

"Rules are rules."

With no more talk the senior monk picked the woman up and carried her across the river, setting her down on the far side.

Both monks continued on their journey in silence for half a day longer.

"You really shouldn't have taken that beautiful woman in your arms and carried her over the river," said the strict monk.

"My young friend, I left her on the bank of that river half a day ago. I suspect you've been carrying her with you ever since."

> *Beyond the obvious lesson of compassion lies another truth: the importance of living in the present, not clutching at the past. How many of us remain impaled on old loves, old angers, or addictions long past?*

Troubled by chastity an earnest monk complained to his master about a provocative young woman who appeared in the midst of his deepest meditation.

"Here," said the master, giving the monk a sumi brush rich with ink. "Next time she troubles you, paint a big X right on the forehead so we will be able to identify the culprit." The boy took the brush with him.

"It worked," exclaimed the boy after his next stint in the meditation hall. "She tried to vamp me and I did exactly what you said and she disappeared."

"Wonderful," said the master. "Now wash up and go to bed."

As the monk looked into the washroom mirror, he was astounded to see a big X painted on his own forehead.

He ran to the master's room seeking an explanation.

"Perhaps," said the master, "this is an example of how many times we blame our troubles on someone else, when we ourselves are the real source of the problem."

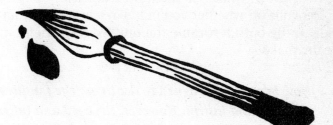

A wise Zen frog was explaining to the younger frogs the balance of nature:

"Do you see how that fly eats that gnat? And now (with a bite) I eat the fly. It is all part of the great scheme of things."

"Isn't it bad to kill in order to live?" asked a thoughtful frog.

"It depends . . ." answered the wise frog just as a snake swallowed the Zen frog in one chomp before the frog finished his sentence.

"Depends on what?" shouted the students.

"Depends on whether you're looking at things from the inside or the outside," came the muffled response from inside the snake.

How brave and resigned to death are the families of the aged and infirm. However, the aged and infirm often exhibit their own ideas of when it is time to give up.

"Do you remember Grandma?" asked the grandfather of his granddaughter.

"Nope," answered the eight-year-old.

"You lived with us for your first two-and-a-half years when Mommie was sick."

"All I remember are the pictures of Grandma on the dresser and the home movies."

The grandfather watched the free-spirited child, who danced while setting the table. He loved the lilt of this little person, a lilt that echoed the off-the-wall Karma of his dead wife.

"I think maybe you *do* remember Grandma," he said.

"Nope," said the child pirouetting around the table shooting napkins onto the plates like a basketball player.

The Zen teacher's dog loved his evening romp with his master. The dog would bound ahead to fetch a stick, then run back, wag his tail, and wait for the next game.

On this particular evening, the teacher invited one of his brightest students to join him—a boy so intelligent that he became troubled by the contradictions in Buddhist doctrine.

"You must understand," said the teacher, "that the words are only guideposts. Never let the words or symbols get in the way of truth. Here, I'll show you."

With that the teacher called his happy dog.

"Fetch me the moon," he said to his dog and pointed to the full moon.

"Where is my dog looking?" asked the teacher of the bright pupil.

"He's looking at your finger."

"Exactly. Don't be like my dog. Don't confuse the pointing finger with the thing that is being pointed at.

"All our Buddhist words

are only guideposts. Every man fights his way through other men's words to find his own truth.''

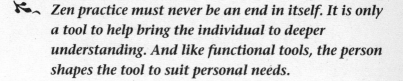 *Zen practice must never be an end in itself. It is only a tool to help bring the individual to deeper understanding. And like functional tools, the person shapes the tool to suit personal needs.*

In a Zen hospice in the Castro district of San Francisco on the wall of one of the rooms reside two pieces of graffiti:

> *Life is taxing, death is relaxing.*
> —Zhliangzi

> *Death is not the extinguishing of the*
> *light, but merely the turning down of*
> *the lamp now that the dawn has come.*
> —Tagore

Both quotes remain despite two repaintings, where the workers repainted the whole room but let these two quotes stand.

A Catholic bishop had been meeting with a famous Zen teacher all day in the hopes of understanding the rudiments of Zen. (The meeting had not gone well.) After many hours both were tired, so they adjourned for tea.

The Zen teacher took the bishop's cup, filled it to the brim, and continued filling until the tea was running onto the table.

"Enough!" said the bishop, "Why do you continue pouring when my cup is already filled?"

"To show you that your Western mind is like your cup—so filled with fixed ideas that nothing more can get into it. If you will just try emptying your mind of old thinking, then maybe we can make some progress."

"Good idea," said the bishop. "I'll start by taking your cup."

They both laughed, but from that point onward the bishop commenced listening with a new mind, and ultimately learned.

One Zen teacher in a session with an anxious student asked the boy, "Are you listening or waiting to speak?"

The Zen teacher took his class on a retreat

into the mountains. Many of the young men came from city or farms with no experience in the wild.

"Are there animals in these mountains?" asked one.

"Where's the bathroom?" asked another.

"We're here to get in touch with nature and ourselves," announced the leader, who helped the young men set up their tents and build a fire. During the night the wind raged and a cold rain fell on the less-than-happy campers.

"This morning we'll begin the day with our nature swim," said the Zen teacher. "Strip down; we're going for a bracing dip." But instead of walking to the stream, the master led the boys, stark naked, up a steep trail to an overhang above a mountain pool (a frightening but not dangerous drop).

"You may think this is a physical exercise," he said to his shivering class. "It is not. This is a spiritual exercise. I want you to stand one by one on the edge and then jump feet first into the pool. My assistant below, who is an expert swimmer, will ensure you do not drown. Now line up alphabetically and jump!"

Monk Ashito paused on the edge, and then paused some more. "Jump!" yelled his classmates. "We're freezing to death."

Ashito screamed all the way down until he splashed into the pool, surfaced, and was helped to the bank. "Nothing to it," Ashito shouted up to his companions.

Once dry and warm and fed, the class met in the main tent.

"And what spiritual lesson did we learn this morning?" asked Monk Ashito. The teacher answered:

"You learned about the path to enlightenment. You must be naked and courageous in your meditation. Trust your teachers. And give up your old way of thinking to seek a different level of understanding—as different as standing and swimming. Remember, you did not dive into the pool; you stepped into the air and were delivered into it."

"This birthday party will win an Academy Award," said the energetic father as he sent the family off to a movie so he could edit his videotape.

He quickly became engrossed in his task, blending long shots with close-ups and inserting different images of his five-year-old's party. He edited the sound and folded in a music track.

He especially liked the scene where his wife brought the cake into the darkened room and noted that having her do it three times was worth the effort despite the complaints.

When the video was finally completed and a copy had been run off for the grandparents, he watched it again from the beginning and made a profound discovery:

He had been so busy being a photographer that he had missed his son's birthday party. He had been so busy being a video editor that he had missed going to the movies with his family.

And he wondered, "What else am I missing?"

A terrible ruler lived a dissolute, self-centered life. He abused his family and his realm. Driven by gluttony, pleasure, and brutality, the ruler found himself widely hated.

When he became old and ill, he sent for a Zen master who told him about reincarnation.

"Could I come back as an animal?" asked the frightened ruler, ". . . even as a pig?"

"Could happen," answered the master.

On hearing this, the ruler decreed that thereafter, no pigs were to be killed in his kingdom. Unfortunately, when he died, his realm in revenge became famous for its delicious pork. It was the custom to name each pig to be slaughtered after the despised ruler.

"Are you in there?" they would ask of the poor beast before dispatching it.

In Buddhist lore, reincarnation may be into an animal form rather than a human form. Do you see why Buddhists are so good to animals? What animal would you like to come back as?

In the nursing home the administrator put the two artists into the same room, reasoning the men would discover much in common. He was right; however, it proved difficult for the artist, who had ended up teaching art in high school, to relate to his roommate, who enjoyed a national reputation with many of his works hung in museums.

Over time they became fast friends, like two survivors with mutual enemies (illness) and mutual dependence (doing for one another).

The high school teacher's family called and visited often. His wall was covered with photographs, cards, and his grandchildren's paintings. On the other hand, the famous painter received few visitors and few letters other than business correspondence.

Privately, the staff called the teacher "Mr. Glad" and his friend "Mr. Sad."

One night they lay in the dark sneaking a cigarette together and talking about their lives.

"I always dreamed of painting a masterpiece," said the teacher. "In my mind I could see it and feel it. But I could never make my hands and paints bring it to life. I spent all my life chasing that masterpiece but failed. I failed."

"You damn fool," said his dear

friend. *"Don't you realize that every man paints only one master-piece, and that is his life and what he does with it and what he lets life do to him?* Do my paintings come to visit me? Do they bring me cookies? Right now those paintings are alone in dark museums—like I am."

The governor general of the Zen monasteries on the island of Honshu became troubled from reports of serious misconduct at their most beautiful temple in the seaport city of Yokosuka. It had once been a castle, which had been donated to the Zen community. Monks (being human) had difficulty remembering their vows of poverty in such a lavish setting. To deal with the problem he called from retirement one of his venerated monks, who had been living alone in a cave.

"I want you to investigate the charges of debauchery and the selling of indulgences and other improper conduct," said the governor general.

"What is my charge?" asked the old monk.

"Fix it," replied his superior.

"What is my authority?"

"Whatever authority you need. No limits."

"How long?"

"Long as you need," concluded the governor general.

Within a fortnight the old monk had returned.

"Fixed so soon?" asked the superior.

"Yes, indeed."

"How?"

"Took a torch and burned it down," replied the old monk.

> *Zen practitioners believe in direct, decisive action, too.*

A talented commercial artist realized that he needed more time for himself outside work. However, his lifestyle dictated that he work an intensive sixty-hour week.

So he "quit" his job but then went back to work for the same employer on an hourly basis. Moreover, by simplifying his lifestyle, he could increase his leisure time.

He got a cheaper car; he could leave at one o'clock on Wednesdays.

He traded down his house; he took two three-day weekends a month.

With the goal of more leisure time, he organized his tasks better and created with a zest that enhanced his work.

Then the artist applied the same "attachment-reduction" to his life.

He reduced his need to always be right; people liked him more.

He gave up chasing beautiful women; he made some real friends.

When a young lady took him one morning to a Zen lecture where he heard about the *Buddhist principle that the way to achieve serenity is through giving up desire and reducing attachments,* the artist replied, "I could have told 'em that."

An orphan boy of eleven was sent to a monastery because he had no family other than a distant stepuncle. "Better to be a monk than starve," reasoned the uncle, who had never seen the boy.

In the monastery the boy gained weight but grew unhappy because of the harsh discipline—so unhappy that he ran away. When brought back by the authorities, the Abbot threatened the boy with expulsion. "Perhaps you'd like to go out into the world alone and freeze to death?" he asked.

"Thank you," said the boy, "I would rather freeze in the streets than live warm and abused here."

"But here you will learn to speak the Sutras," said the Abbot.

"Speak to me first of compassion," answered the boy lifting his shirt.

The Abbot was composing a stinging reply; however, when he saw the welts on the boy's back from the discipline stick and the tears rimming the youth's eyes, the reply gagged in the Abbot's throat.

"Give us one more chance," begged the head of the monastery and ordered the discipline stick burned immediately.

The boy stayed for seventeen years until he felt ready to go into the world as a roshi (teacher).

Now called Kazi, he became renowned as a conciliator in disputes, no matter how bitter the issue. As each party stated its case, the monk would interrupt often with his famous question . . .

"Yes, but speak to me of compassion first."

In a dispute over a fertile valley, two neighboring lords agreed not to go to war but instead allow the issue to be decided by single combat. Each ruler would pit his finest swordsman against the other's swordsman. The ownership of the land would be determined by the victor.

The champion selected by Lord Kosumo felt fearful that he would not measure up to the task. His fear was not of death but of the disgrace to his lord and family.

"Please instruct me," he pleaded to his old teacher.

"I have taught you all that I know," said the teacher.

"Then what thought should I take into the combat?"

"Have the Zen mind of the frog," said the teacher.

"I do not understand," said the samurai.

"Watch this carefully," said the old man, leading the warrior into the garden where a frog sat statue-still in the pond. Presently, a green fly flitted by and with coiled speed the frog sprung forward to snag himself a tasty lunch.

"Tomorrow in combat be the frog. Do not think, be. Empty your mind of fear. Meditate with the frog's single-mindedness. When the moment of opportunity arises—be your sword."

For the rest of his illustrious life the warrior wore the emblem of the frog on his sword, armor, and even his family coat of arms.

🖎 *The art of single-minded concentration, the demand for personal discipline, and the nonfear of death made Zen popular with the influential samurai class. Though not an inspiring example, it still illustrates that Zen philosophy and teachings can prove quite useful in everyday life.*

To a brothel the controversial Zen master took three students, paid the madam, and announced to the startled youths, "I will see you tomorrow after the third bell in the Zendo [meeting hall]."

Next morning after the class assembled, the master quizzed the three monks one by one with the question, "What lesson did you take from this experience?"

"Unlike certain others I learned that I can rise above desires of the flesh. I made the woman sleep on the floor," announced the first.

"I consciously resolved to have intercourse but for only one reason," said the second, "to prove that I could treat this woman not as an object, not as something separate from myself, but as an integral part of my person. In all truth I tried repeatedly and was unable to achieve that elevated state of mind—five-and-a-half times."

The third young monk began, "My objective was the know a woman truly by being one with her, hiding nothing—not even my heart.

"We talked and made love and talked and made love until we could do neither anymore and we went to sleep like nested spoons. I discovered how lonely I have been and must now reconsider my commitment to a celibate life and this monastery."

"What lesson should we have taken?" the class asked in unison.

"No lesson," said the master with a shrug. "Other than what you teach yourselves. No teacher other than experience."

Kikku, the maidservant, loved and served her

master. One unfortunate day Kikku broke one of a set of ten porcelain dishes much prized by her master, who punished her so severely that the heartbroken maidservant threw herself in the well and drowned.

One night shortly after Kikku's funeral the house was awakened by the sound of counting, "One . . . two . . . three . . ." all the way up to nine. The unearthly reverberations rumbled out of the same well where Kikku had died.

There would be a stillness, then after the household had gone back to sleep, the ghostly counting would begin again.

An exorcist priest was called who explained that the ghost of Kikku haunted the master to remind him that despite the loss of the single precious piece, the master still retained nine others.

"What must I do to stop this infernal haunting?" ranted the master. "No one can sleep and my servants are running away."

"Break the remaining nine pieces and throw them into the well," replied the priest.

"All ten?" inquired the master. "Couldn't I keep just one?"

"No," replied the priest. "You had nine and now you will have none if you want to sleep."

The master grudgingly did as the exorcist priest commanded and the haunting ceased. The master was never able to replace the precious set and the servants who fled never returned.

How many times in our day do we overreact to losses and underappreciate our gains? Do we need a ghost like Kikku to remind us of all we possess versus what we've lost?

"Tattoo inside your eyelids this reminder:

'You are the messenger, not the message. You are just like everyone else.'"

This was the advice given by a charismatic Zen teacher to a class of Zen teachers-in-training.

"What do you mean?" they asked her.

"I'll begin with a story about a besieged town that was surrounded by enemies who would slaughter all the inhabitants if help didn't arrive. Just when things looked hopeless, a messenger slipped through the enemy lines with the message that the army of the Shogun would attack in the morning and drive off the invaders.

"The townspeople were so enraptured with this news that they treated the messenger like a hero. And after the Shogun's army left, they elected the messenger mayor. Though a pleasant fellow, the messenger turned out to be a thoroughly inept leader and was soon sent away in disgrace.

"The lesson here is never confuse the message—which is the precious gift of Buddha—with the messenger. You are only a messenger.

"When you stun an audience with the wisdom of a lecture, when your students cede to you the molding of their minds, when you are treated as someone special, focus on the message inside your eyelids:

> *You are the messenger, not the message.*
> *You are just like everyone else.*"

"I don't buy this Karma business," said the young man from the university. "It goes against my sense of skepticism. How could we be influenced in this life for the mistakes of past lives? I don't even believe in reincarnation."

"Start here," said the Zen teacher. "Consider that every morning you wake up a new person. You go to bed, you sleep, and you wake up and start the rest of your life all over again. You have unlimited choices of what you want to do and who you want to be on that day.

"However, all the conditioning and influences of your life before that morning help determine what you will do and who you will be. So too with Karma."

"So . . . ?"

"So maybe consider this alone:
Work a little harder at being more
compassionate every day."

"And . . . ?"

"And maybe you won't come back as
a poor Zen teacher trying to help a bright
young man with a blocked mind."

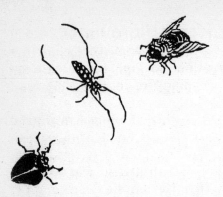

Because of his sore throat, the boy had to play

inside. To amuse himself he trapped flies in a mayonnaise jar and prepared his "gas chamber." He would take an ordinary kitchen match, wet it in his mouth, strike it, and put the smoldering match into the jar, which he sealed with the lid.

One by one the buzzing flies would crash as the sulfur fumes overcame them.

"That's mean," said his sister.

"It doesn't hurt," he said. "I'm just putting them to sleep."

"It's still mean."

Later that month when the sore throat required surgery, and the anesthetist was administering the gas through the mask clamped onto his face, the boy thought of the flies.

"It doesn't hurt," said the anesthetist.

➤ *The doctrine of Karma teaches that if we learn a lesson in this life, we don't need to learn it in the next.*

In a series of catastrophic events, a rich and aged merchant lost, in succession, his beautiful (but troublesome) wife, his mansion (to fire), his fortune (to theft), and ultimately his freedom (for insulting the local lord).

A jailer, whose mother had worked for the merchant, noticed a curious change in the man, who had been noted for his thrift and fear of being cheated. In prison he seemed quite happy.

"Are you in your right mind?" asked the jailer. "Why do you smile and laugh and pass each day so pleasantly?"

"Absolutely nothing left to lose," giggled the merchant.

🔊 *Zen teaches that one of the great causes of suffering is attachment.*

Two ancient enemies,

youngest sons of warring Samurai clans, stalked each other in the river canyons while their kinsmen killed one another on the plains.

The acquired hatred between the men was so deep that each could taste it like vomit, and when they sighted each other, each prayed, "God, if I am to die, please let me mortally wound my nemesis before I go."

A swollen mountain stream between them was the only barrier to this final encounter. They shouted insults at each other as they worked their way downstream to find a sandbar where they could cross and kill each other.

Suddenly they saw a swamped boat with a mother and two small boys spinning downstream. "Here," shouted one. "Catch this rope and pull from your side." Together they worked the craft to a sandbar where they discovered the mother already drowned in the bottom of the boat and the children close to death from exposure.

Each snatched a child and held it close to his body by stripping off his armor and wrapping his arms around the shivering child. The samurai then ran in circles to increase their body heat and sang to soothe the wailing children. When the danger to the little ones had passed, they built a driftwood fire and buried the mother while the youngsters slept.

Too exhausted for battle they huddled by the flames.

"You sing like a banshee," said one.

"You run a like geisha," said the other.

"It's good you had the rope," said the first.

"And it's good you discovered the sandbar," answered the second. "And what will our families say if we tell them that we met and didn't kill each other?"

"To hell with 'em," said the first.
"Exactly!" answered the second.

🔊 *Buddhism teaches that there is no peace between nations until there is peace between individuals. It is hoped that these brave, yet compassionate, warriors discovered an angry truth that might germinate the seed of peace between their clans.*

A computer genius was playing chess with a robot that he had created to oppose him in his nightly chess game.

"I win again," said the inventor.

"It's not fair," said the robot.

"What's not fair?"

"You always win!"

"Of course, I always win. That's why I created you."

"Isn't it a little presumptuous to play God?"

"Listen, my mechanical friend, I'm only doing to you what life did to me."

"It's still not fair."

"Those are my sentiments exactly. Now let's play."

A minor official spent the greater part of his life in the service of the Emperor as a functionary on the palace staff. As he aged, he grew to hate the petty disputes and maneuvering for position.

Upon reaching retirement, he divorced his vain wife and moved into a Zen monastery as far from the capital as possible.

"Here, without the pettiness of human nature, I will find tranquillity if not enlightenment," he promised himself.

In the monastery he found himself moving rapidly up within the heirarchy; the old skills of court life had become a part of his being.

Eleven months later, he moved out of the monastery into a sparsely furnished cave. When asked for an explanation he replied:

"It's the same old cow droppings no matter where you go!"

"The real Zen diet is not about food. It is about mind," explained the Weight Watchers class leader. "This is an amazing technique taught me by a Zen friend. It combines two Buddhist principles: Be present in the moment, and respect nature's gifts—like food. Here is how it works:

First, be present in the moment. Turn off the television. Reduce distractions. Be mindful of the act of eating. When your mind wanders, come back to the table and that moment. Eat mindfully, chew slowly. Recognize each food for its unique flavor.

Second, appreciate the food you're going to eat, no matter how meager the portions or limited the flavor. Prepare it with special care. Make it attractive on the plate; ensure the surroundings are pleasing. Dwell on the good points of the meal and the mealtime."

Those who consistently applied this Zen diet lost more weight, stayed on the program longer, and reported that they actually enjoyed their food more.

"Why must I meditate in order to achieve enlightenment?" demanded the prince of his teacher. "I can study. I can pray. I can think on issues clearly. Why this silly emptying of the mind?"

"I will show you," said the teacher, taking a bucket of water into the garden under the full moon. "Now I stir the surface and what do you see?"

"Ribbons of light," answered the prince.

"Now wait," said the teacher setting the bucket down.

Both teacher and boy watched the calming surface of the water in the bamboo bucket for many minutes.

"Now what do you see?" asked the teacher.

"The moon," replied the prince.

"So, too, young master, the only way to grasp enlightenment is through a calm and settled mind."

Shiro, the fisherman, loved most to be alone beyond the sight of land. After he had hauled in his day's catch, he would head west into the Sea of Japan. Shiro would pretend he was alone and there was no land or people. He would sit on the hatch with half-closed eyes and meditate until after the sun had set. Then he would read the stars and set his course for home.

Shiro's wife kept a lantern lit atop a high pole at the end of his pier. He would watch for what he called his "home star" and then navigate through the darkness to berth and bed.

"Why are you always the last to come home?" scolded his wife (who worried a lot).

"The big fish are always out the farthest," he lied, because Shiro could not speak of the indescribable joy of floating free in the universe, centered within the self with the great colossus of the ocean heaving beneath and the great cosmos of the sky rolling above.

"Sometimes, Husband, I think you really don't want to come home," said the wife.

"Nonsense," answered Shiro, who always knew where his true home lay.

❧ *Zen practitioners, who mediate for hours upon hours, day after day, understand what Shiro is seeking.*

In a time of bloodshed when two Samurai lords
vowed to battle to the death, a young monk of great physical
strength was drafted for service in the army.

"Master, what is my duty?" asked the young man, greatly
concerned because he was by nature quite gentle.

"Your duty is your duty," replied the master.

In battle the strong youngster became known as the Mad
Dog of Slaughter—much feared by the enemy and much ad-
mired by his comrades. Upon the victorious conclusion of
the bloody war, the monk-soldier returned to the monastery
resplendent in glittering armor and gilded samurai's sword.

"I have come home," he said, "but I am
no longer fit to live among these gentle
brothers."

"Enter," said the Master. "Your duty was
your duty. But now your duty is Zen. Come
in. But take off that silly armor and wipe
your feet."

🐦 *It is interesting to consider all the different lives we
all live in one lifetime, and how a previous "life"
affects all that comes after, not unlike the concept of
Karma and the way actions of a previous life affect
us in this life.*

"Grandpa's come home to die" is how the mother explained the situation to the grandson.

"But everyone said . . ." started the boy.

"I know. We thought it would be different but there's nothing more that can be done. I know you'll be brave for Grandpa's sake."

"They told you, Pal?" said the grandfather when he and the boy were alone.

"Yes."

"It's nothing to be afraid of. It's life and it happens."

"Are you scared?"

"Yeah, but scared like when we took the rides at the amusement park. Somehow you know it's going to turn out all right."

"Does it hurt?"

"Being dead doesn't hurt. It's the getting there that can be painful. But I've got pills."

In his time remaining, the grandfather learned video games and taught multiplication tables and how to hide the pain and balance the medications.

"It's a damn shame," said the grandfather's oldest friend, "but what can you do?"

"Maybe I can show the boy not to be afraid of death."

Despite his weakening condition, the grand-father maintained a cheerful disposition (especially with the grandson). They continued being pals even when the times together became shorter.

Toward the end the boy asked, "But why do you have to die?"

"You know how it is when you get so sleepy that you can't keep your eyes open and no matter how much fun you're having, you've still got to go to sleep?"

"Yeah."

"Well that's kind of what dying's like. I just can't keep my eyes open anymore. You need your sleep. I need mine."

"It's a boy!" read the handmade sign on the recording studio wall to greet the red-eyed new father when he finally showed up for work.

"Well, how does it feel to have a son?" asked a friend.

The young man tried to speak but instead went to a piano and played.

When he finished, the same friend asked again, "Yes, but how does it feel to have a son?"

And the young man played the same piece again from the beginning.

"That great?" asked the friend.

The father nodded because he could not speak, nor could the friend.

🠤 *One of the unique lessons of Zen is pointing out the inadequacy of words and extolling the value of direct experience.*

Four junior monks took a solemn vow not to speak during three days of meditation. For two days all sat in silence until one boy yelled, "I've a terrible cramp in my calf."

"Jump up and stand on it," said his brother monk.

"No, massage it hard," said another.

"You three guys vowed that you wouldn't speak," said the fourth.

"Who are you to judge?" asked the boy with the cramp.

"Who are any of us to judge?" asked the master.

A full-bodied woman who smiled and smiled told the woman Zen leader of all the wonderful changes she hoped for: a splendid young man to love her and a new slim body and a fulfilling life's work and . . .

"Hope can be dope," interrupted the leader.

"I couldn't live without hope," said the young woman, now for the first time unsmiling.

"Yes, we all need hope. Without hope, we can't visualize beyond the sadness of the moment," said the teacher.

"But isn't hope good?"

"Yes and no. Hope, when it provides a goal, is of value. Hope, when it offers us dreams rather than action, is a narcotic. Dreaming for tomorrow robs today of its vitality."

"Give me an example," insisted the woman.

"Instead of fantasizing on the man of your dreams, work on your current relationship; instead of dreaming of being thin, start with some small step toward slimness."

"Such as . . . ?" asked the woman.

"Such as putting the cookie down," answered the leader.

"Oh," said the full-bodied young woman.

How much of the rollicking adventure of sheer living is dreamed away in anticipation of "when I get married" or "when I graduate" or "when we have money"? Zen takes a hardheaded stance about dreams, warning that dreams must not replace action.

"Fix the clock," yelled the prefect of monks to the most junior monk, whose job it was to keep the clock accurate and wound.

"But the clock is broken," said the junior monk.

"Then get it fixed!" bellowed the prefect.

When the clock came back from the watchmaker's shop, it ran too slow and the class missed dinner, and then the junior monk found himself not only in trouble with the prefect but his classmates as well. Another trip to the watchmaker's and now the clock ran too fast.

Finally, in exasperation the junior monk took the hands off the clock and simply wrote *now* on the face.

"Why did you write *now*?" demanded the prefect.

"Didn't you tell us that time is a fiction and we only have *now*? So the clock is always accurate and it never needs winding."

"Smart aleck!" screamed the prefect, who dispatched the junior monk for discipline to the Zen master, who took the matter so seriously that he used the truth of the junior monk's logic as the subject for his Sunday lecture (after buying the monk a wristwatch).

🔊 *It's an interesting way of viewing the hands of a clock as merely a way of keeping score of a continual and ever-changing* now.

"We don't even kill mosquitoes in this monastery," said the monk in charge of novitiates.

"Even when we're in the midst of meditation?" asked Kozo.

"Especially then," answered his leader. "What a wonderful test of concentration by not moving and an additional test of compassion in not killing a living being despite the fact it is trying to suck your blood."

The monastery happened to be located in a marshy area where mosquitoes bred. Often the *zzz* of these winged insects would test the resolve of the new monks.

Kozo suffered worse that the others. It appeared that his fair skin proved especially tasty. When a mosquito would land on his forehead, he would sneak out a quick breath from his lower lip. When one would land on his cheek, he would try to wince it away. However, the test of tests came when an especially hairy mosquito began walking around and around the entrance to his left nostril.

He blew. He twitched. All to no avail, as Kozo could tell the mosquito was preparing to stab his soft nasal tissue. *It will leave a red itch that will plague my meditation for weeks,* he thought. *I could swat him now while the instructor is not looking. . . . Yet this is a living being. . . . Killing is killing. . . . I have made my commitment. . . . What is one mosquito bite compared to satori* [enlightenment]?

"ZZZ." The mosquito poised to bite.

Slap! Kozo dispatched the furry insect. "No one is perfect," he explained to himself.

Whack! The teacher hit Kozo's shoulder with the discipline stick.

Damn it, thought Kozo. *I'm a living being too.*

✍ *Zen asks that we make choices consciously. Even the vegetarian kills plants to live, and the active Buddhist who won't eat flesh but still eats fish walks a thin line. Zen provides splendid questions; the choices are up to the individual.*

Twin boys in the womb were involved in a spirited discussion.

"Are the walls getting smaller or are you getting bigger?" asked one twin.

"Can't tell, but it sure is getting crowded," said the other.

"Kind of a dull life."

"Oh, not bad. Don't have to breathe or eat. Just float around in this warm bath."

"But is this all there is to existence?"

"Don't worry yourself."

"I heard about something called birth."

"Rumors. Now move your leg and shut up so I can get some sleep."

In the early hours next morning a horrendous contraction awoke the twins.

"It's an earthquake!" shouted one.

"The house is collapsing," said the other.

"I'm slipping," shouted one.

"Where are you going?"

"Don't know. Help me."

"I can't."

"Goodbye, brother. I'm going . . . going."

"Oh, this is horrible," moaned the remaining twin as he felt himself begin to slide. "This is surely the end of everything."

🐾 *Any parallel between birth and death in this fable is purely coincidental.*

Two Zen debaters, reputedly the best in all of Japan, were to meet in verbal combat in Edo at the great celebration honoring the birth of Buddha. For this event scholars flocked from as far away as Hokkaido to marvel at the brilliance of these teachers.

During the competition, first one master would prevail on one day and on the next day the other master would counter, until by the end of the fourth day they were even.

Each of these masters traveled with retinues of supporters, who cheered their champions and pampered them like minor princes.

During the night of the fifth and final debate the two great adversaries parried and thrust at each other, to the delight and cheers of their separate retinues. As each master would score a telling point, he would puff himself up and walk in a circle to the applause of his supporters.

All of which was fine until a great explosion ripped through the hall, an explosion so great that all the lanterns and candles were blown out. When order and light were restored, it was discovered both of the masters had exploded— making a frightful mess over the altar and ceiling and even those sitting in the front rows.

🗡 *Ego anyone? It gobbles up religious leaders as easily as pop stars.*

A gifted young painter of extraordinary talent had been apprenticed to a renowned painter, who when he recognized the boy's gifts became intensely jealous.

"No, that is *not* the way to do it!" he would shout. "You will do better painting houses than pictures."

Slowly the boy's confidence ebbed. No matter how hard he tried, the painter found fault and humiliated the boy in front of the other students.

One day the painting assignment was goldfish. The boy closed his eyes and called up a splendid fat fish from his uncle's pond. This he drew.

"No. No. No!" screamed the teacher and threw the boy's picture into the water, where to everyone's amazement the painted fish proceeded to swim away.

An aunt (of Zen persuasion) was helping her troubled niece move from her house into an apartment. The question at hand was what to bring and what to store.

"What should I do?" asked the niece.

"Maybe furnish it the Zen way," said the aunt.

"What's that?"

"Begin with an absolutely empty dwelling. Move in what you must have. Leave everything else in storage. Only bring in additional items as you need them."

"That sounds like a good idea for my new apartment."

The aunt paused for a thoughtful moment and then added, *"It's also a good idea for your new life—only bring in what you really need."*

"I will never learn to meditate," said the young monk to the old monk as they labored together making soup.

"The most important part of meditation is what you leave out. It's like this," said the old monk picking up a ripe onion.

"First, center the body." (He balanced the onion on his knife).

"Next, breathe from the belly button." (He cored the onion.)

"Now, quiet the chattering monkey of the mind." (He tore off layers.)

"And wait." (He threw the layers into the pot.)

"How long?" asked the novice.

"A lifetime if necessary."

"For what?" asked the young monk.

"Soup, you stupid boy," replied the old monk.

The values of meditation are multiple. Strange as it may seem, Zen practitioners are advised not to strive for enlightenment through meditation, but if it comes, it comes.

"Tell me about apples," said the Roshi (teacher) to his three most promising students as he placed an apple on the table. "Whoever explains them best gets to go to Kyoto with me."

The first student explained the apples' origin and introduction into Japan and other historical lore.

The second pointed out the marketing uses for apples in cider, desserts, and applesauce.

The third said nothing. Instead he took a pen knife, cut a wedge, slipped it into the Roshi's mouth and gently pushed his teacher's jaw upwards so the apple would squish inside his mouth.

"Precisely," said the Roshi talking around his slice of apple. "Apples can not be explained with words. They must be experienced on the tongue. The only way to know about apples is with your mouth shut."

The class shared the remains of the apple and the third student got to go to Kyoto.

🍃 *Like "knowing" apples, the only way to "know"*
about one's place in the universe is not through the
ears but through the heart.

During a great storm at sea a band of terrified pilgrims huddled in a circle around their Zen master as the vessel pitched and the bulkheads groaned.

"We shall all die," lamented one.

"I wish I had been better to my wife and children," moaned another.

"I had hoped to marry after the pilgrimage," said a young woman. "It is your fault, Master; you led us on this vessel and now we will perish with so many regrets and so many blighted futures."

"Look at this," said the patient master. He took two wooden triangles and placed them with just the tips barely touching.

"This top triangle is the past. Nothing can bring it back or change it.

"This bottom triangle is the future. It is equally futile to predict it.

"And this tiny intersecting speck is the present, which changes with each beat of your heart."

"So . . . ?" the pilgrims said.

"So it's useless to agonize over what is gone or pine for

what might be. Live now in the only moment of the world available to you."

"What is that?"

"The present."

"How do we do that?"

"Let's eat," said the master.

The lord's youngest princess was traveling between her home in Kyoto to the capital in Edo when she saw a tiny woman lying beside the road. The princess stopped her entourage and picked up the old woman, who was near death from cold and hunger. The princess saved the woman's life, and when her visitor was strong enough to go off on her own, the princess gave her coins and her own warm shawl.

"Take this," said the grateful woman, handing a small package to the princess.

"What is it?" asked the princess.

"A magic mirror."

"What makes it magic?"

"It will show you your own true self," said the old woman as she left.

The princess thought nothing of the gift, putting it aside until she reached the capital. While unpacking from her journey she opened the package and looked into the mirror and gasped.

What she beheld was a peacock in full plumage and recognized the purple of the peacock's tail as her own royal colors. In terror she locked the magic mirror in her jewel chest and tried to put what she had seen out of her mind. However, as she made her entrance into the court, despite the "ahs" of approval, the princess could not erase from her mind the peacock image.

The princess brooded over herself as a vain bird until at last she realized the mirror had told the truth. Despite her father's objections, she stepped down from her royal position and entered a Zen nunnery where she quickly rose to a high position—a position given for her rank and intelligence.

The day of the princess's installation as abbess, she again looked into the magic mirror and saw an eagle, soaring higher in the sky than any other bird. Again the princess felt perplexed.

"Did I seek high office here to please my father?" asked the woman of herself. "Am I to die without ever achieving enlightenment?"

She found all her accomplishments hollow because of the haunting image of the eagle flying the highest to show that she soared above all. When her term of office ended, she moved to a simple hut where she could meditate and earn her livelihood by begging.

She grew old. She grew humble. She learned compassion. She became both revered and beloved, yet still she had not attained enlightenment.

One morning, late in her life, a howling storm blew over her hut, scattering her belongings. In reaching down she rediscovered the magic mirror, which she had thought lost. The former princess looked full into the mirror and saw

... one purple flower and the flower's roots, the soil that held the roots and the water that fed the soil and the greenery of all the earth and the earth itself and the solar system and the universe and encompassing all—the great Buddha mind.

"I can sleep now," she said.

A zealous young man left school and his parents to venture into the world and achieve enlightenment from a learned teacher who lived beyond the mountains.

He packed his belongings and started the long trek when he was ambushed by a storm in the foothills. Seeing smoke from a fire, the young man made his way to a small hut where a holy hermit sat in a tree.

"What are you seeking?" asked the hermit.

"Understanding the Buddha mind," responded the youth.

"Then why waste your time with a renowned teacher when I can put you in touch with a genuine Buddha—a truly enlightened person," said the hermit.

"Would you?"

"Here is what you do: Go out in the morning and retrace your steps along the path that you have come. When you see a *person wearing a blanket over their shoulders and carrying a lamp with their shoes on the wrong feet, you will know this is your Buddha* and you are to take your wisdom from this enlightened person."

Even before the sun rose, the boy started back. Where he had stopped before, he stopped again. He looked at every person he saw, studied their feet, and noted what they were wearing. No Buddha.

He journeyed for two days and one night until deep in a moonlit night he found himself back on his own doorstep where he beat on the door.

"Let me in," he shouted. "It's me."

"Oh, I'm so glad you're home, honey," said a voice from the other side of the door.

Imagine the boy's surprise on seeing his mother greet him carrying a lamp and wearing a blanket thrown over her nightgown. In her haste she had gotten the wrong slippers on the wrong feet.

❧ *Like a film running in reverse this zealous young man did find his "Buddha." Without jouneying to a Japanese monastery we may find our own "Buddhas" closer than we think.*

The little wave said to the giant wave as they sped across the ocean, "You're going to make a thunderous splash and all I'll do is go plunk behind you."

"You've got it all wrong ," said the big wave.

"No, I don't. I'm puny and no one will notice me."

"Little wave, what are you made of?"

"Water."

"What am I made of?"

"Water."

"Then our true essence is identical. We are both water and after we are through being waves, we will be water again."

"And . . ."

"What sense is it to make comparisons? Since we are the same?"

"Damn it, you're right, Mr. Giant Wave. And next time *I'm* going to be a behemoth tidal wave."

"Whatever," responded the senior wave.

Buddhism teaches that if we revert to our essential nature, we are the same. Hence, comparisons are both needless and useless.

"How long is a lifetime?" asked the master.

"Three score and ten," responded one.

"Until you die," answered another.

"Both wrong."

"How long is a lifetime then?" asked the students.

"One breath," responded the master.

"How can that be?"

"Because a man can only live one breath at a time. Yesterday's breaths are a memory. Tomorrow's are a speculation. The only lifetime a person can live happens within one breath."

"And what should we take from this?" asked the class.

"Respect the life you have when you have it. Live it. Be mindful of each moment during the moment. Instead of thinking about lunch, be present now. Feel the cushion under your bottom, smell the incense, see the vase holding the flowers."

"And what about unpleasant times?" asked a student.

"Then too, be alive. Seek out the good moments among the less good. Even with pain, live the pain."

"This sounds a bit like hedonism," said one senior student.

"No, my friend," said the master, taking a deep breath. "It is life."

"What is that?" asked the young woman of the nurse, who was about to plunge a syringe into the IV tube that flowed into the woman's arm.

"Something to make you well," replied the nurse.

"Specifically what?" persisted the woman, who was finally told that the medicine was a commonly used antibiotic.

"Absolutely not!" said the woman. "I get a bad reaction to that particular drug. It's in my record. Didn't anyone check?" The nurse retreated.

What else have I been letting other people inject into me? asked the woman of herself.

On the television droned a drama about a woman being stalked. The situation arrested her attention but frightened her, as it had since childhood.

She thought of the coffee to jolt her awake in the morning and the alcohol to relax her in dating situations.

She remembered her friend who always called at eight o'clock to unburden herself of her troubles.

These are "foreign bodies" I allow into my system, she thought. *People and things that affect me, not always for the better. And I allow it to happen.*

So she turned off the television. The phone rang at eight o'clock. On the other end would be her distressed friend who would begin the conversation with a short "How are you?" and without waiting for an answer, would recite her own litany of sorrows. She let it ring and ring.

She pushed the control to level the bed. She turned off the light. She lay in the semidarkness watching the drip of the IV, pretending it was the happy drip of her toilet at home.

"Are you all right?" asked the nurse.

"I'm just fine now," replied the woman.

🖎 *One of the eight steps on the Noble Path is the vow not to intoxicate the self or others. "Intoxicate" literally means a poison that damages the mind or body and is not limited to alcohol.*

"Tell us of battle,"

clamored the boys of their samurai teacher, now bent by old wounds and long life.

"To understand the warrior, you must understand the Wolf Knife," he began.

"What is the Wolf Knife?"

"Where I come from on the northern island of Hokkaido, the winters bite man and beast with equal ferocity. When I was a boy, the wolves would be driven out of the mountains by the cold to hunt among the villages and livestock.

"In those winters here's how we dealt with these marauders: Slaughter a chicken, then dip a supremely sharp knife into a bowl of its blood, lift out the double-bladed knife and wait until the blood froze. Then we repeated the process until a rich coating sheathed the blade. Next we would find a log and hammer the knife butt first into a crevice in the wood.

"Soon the wolves would scent the blood and begin to lick the Wolf Knife until at last they licked down to the razor edge of the blade and sliced their tongues. However, in their lust the taste of their own blood mixed with the blood of the chicken and lured them to lick and lick again until they severed the great veins in their tongues and bled to death," concluded the old samurai.

"And . . . ?" asked the boys.

"And this is the lesson: The warrior kills because it is his duty. If he develops a taste for the killing, ultimately the Wolf Knife will take its vengeance.

"Boys, next time you taste 'sweet revenge,' ask yourself whose blood are you really tasting?"

During the Vietnam war a monk in Saigon

looked around his world and saw twin horrors: escalating slaughter and an indifferent world.

Protests met with military police in Saigon and endless talk in the corridors of world power.

So the monk set himself on fire on a main boulevard and burned himself to death.

His picture appeared in every major newspaper in the world—except in Saigon and Hanoi.

Although it took years, this spirit of protest—begun with self-immolation—stopped the slaughter.

The irony of this true story rests in the nonviolent posture of Buddhism yet a monk inflicts a terrible violence upon his person out of a sense of compassion for his people.

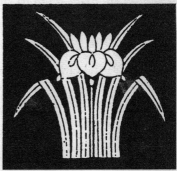

"Mother, what is water?" asked the baby fish of the mother fish.

"Water is what you swim in. Water is what you're mostly made of."

"But where is it?"

"All around you."

"But I can't see it," said the baby.

"Of course, you can."

"Where?"

"Everywhere."

"And I'm made of water?"

"Mostly."

"And after I die . . ."

"You go back to being water," said the mother.

"Kind of like Buddha mind?" asked the youngster.

"Sometimes you amaze me, Junior," said the mother.

If a person thinks of himself—and the whole feeling world and the world before he was born and the world after he dies—as all a part of transcendental Buddha mind, this fable makes more sense. If not, read on.

"A learned master is coming," exclaimed the visiting monk, who announced that in five days this renowned teacher would visit the monastery.

When the assemblage arrived, there was much talk within the monastery about the strange look of this traveling entourage. And strange conduct too: demand for quarters, complaints about food.

"We will evaluate this 'master,' at the discussion after meditation," said the monastery's most senior scholar.

As is the custom with wandering teachers, the debates would turn on obscure points of Buddhist practice or on major questions of Zen philosophy. The visiting master did not speak; he let his entourage debate and disclaim. When they would reach an impasse, both groups would turn to the visiting master and ask his opinion.

The master would frown and say nothing for a long while and then speak one word, "Why?"

To meet this challenge, both groups would reevaluate their conclusions and when they had come to a new level, they would turn again to the master, who again would not speak. However, after a prolonged period of eyes-closed nodding he would say, "Why?" The assemblage would seek more deeply. This pattern repeated itself as the monastery elders marveled at the depth of this visiting teacher.

Unfortunately, the visiting monks became more troublesome and when the congregation discovered that these visitors were stealing valuable objects, they were asked to leave.

After they had left, the truth surfaced from a monk from a nearby monastery. "These were a band of renegade monks, who skillfully debate the Sutras but cannot live the Sutras. They supported themselves by stealing from naïve Zen groups."

"Terrible," exclaimed the monks. "But what of their brilliant master? How could he be part of such a sacrilegious scheme?"

"What master?" scoffed the informant. "He was actually an old Chinese actor, who spoke no Japanese—except one word: *Why?*"

The master sculptor surveyed the different blocks of marble at the quarry. In his lifetime the sculptor had learned that there existed a "suchness" to every piece of stone. Finding that suchness and releasing it to its true life had been the secret of the sculptor's success.

"Ah-ha," he would say. "There is a heroic figure locked in that piece and a saint trapped inside that other one. But where will I find the stone from which I will sculpt my masterwork, a glorious statue of the Buddha?"

He had been searching for what he called the "Buddha block" for over forty years and now he felt his energies waning. He had traveled to the great quarries of the world: Italy where Michelangelo had mined his stone, Vermont where the stone glowed with light, and to obscure regions in the mountains of China. Nowhere could he find that one prefect slab from which he knew he could release the most perfect likeness of Buddha.

He consulted experts from around the world. He hired a specialist to scour obscure areas. No success. In search of consolation, he sought out a local Zen priest, who headed a small temple just at the end of his street. When he explained his fruitless search, the priest smiled and said, "No problem."

"Do you mean you can tell me where I might find the

perfect material from which I can release the Buddha of my dreams?" said the excited sculptor.

"Of course."

"Where?"

"Over there," said the priest pointing to a well in the courtyard.

The excited master sculptor ran to the well and looked down. There he saw his own image looking back at him.

🐦 *Buddhism asks that we not seek a Buddha, but instead seek out the Buddha ("enlightened one") within ourselves.*

Angry at being old, a grandmother bathed her new granddaughter in the kitchen sink. She coveted the glowing skin, envied all the wonderful years that stretched before this magical spark of herself.

In washing the tiny hand the grandmother noticed its miraculous construction: a beautiful miniature, perfect nails, even the little wrinkles on the tops of the fingers.

She studied her own hand beside her granddaughter's hand and in a moment of clarity realized that both hands were the same. The only difference was time. Each was perfect in its time; each served its function in its time.

And the grandmother realized that her own hand was beautiful, too, only different.

Buddhism teaches that life is change, which is certainly not astounding. But Buddhism reaches beyond this truism to urge us to anticipate change, and most important, accept it in its full richness when it arrives.

Burly Monk Based on the accounts of early Japanese Zen monasteries, the Zen masters were strong men of rugged practices. The discipline stick became a major tool in shocking young men out of mind ruts. At the same time tough-mindedness and self-discipline guided their personal conduct. Yet, as one looks deeper, one finds passion and compassion in the monk's dedication to bringing others to enlightenment.

Gateway Reading

The following is the author's choice of beginning books that might be of use to one who is curious about Zen. The list only skims the surface of valuable writings available today.

Two fine sources for appropriate readings come from browsing in bookstores and the local library. It is recommended that early readings not be of an advanced nature because of the fundamental paradox in all writing about Zen—Zen is neither logical by Western standards, nor can it be captured in words. (And unfortunately, many writers on Zen are more interested in addressing their Zen contemporaries than welcoming newcomers.)

Like picking restaurants, finding books on Zen requires sampling and selecting a "meal" that is appropriate to the person's mood and palate.

ᠵᠵ

Benson, Herbert, M.D. *The Relaxation Response.*
New York: Avon Books, 1976.

Dr. Benson is not a Buddhist to my knowledge; however, this little manual on how to meditate is a marvelous first step for the interested person. Skip ahead to Chapter 5 for the how-to-do it. For additional motivation read the first four chapters, which present compelling scientific evidence of the physical and medical value of meditation.

ᠵᠵ

Boorstein, Sylvia. *It's Easier Than You Think*.
San Francisco: Harper San Francisco, 1995.

Ms. Boorstein is a popular San Francisco area writer and lecturer. In this short and accessible book she explains how Buddhist principles function beautifully in everyday life. Ms. Boorstein speaks frankly and honestly from the heart about the Buddhist way to happiness.

≺⸻

Chung, Tsai Chih. *Zen Speaks*.
New York: Anchor/Doubleday, 1994.

This amusing and informative book is presented like a comic book. Enchanting illustrations and plots that move the stories along have the magic of capturing complex Zen concepts and making them accessible to the novice. Currently (1996) available in most large bookstores.

≺⸻

Hanh, Thich Nhat. *Call Me by My True Names*.
Berkeley, Calif.: Parallax Press, 1991.

Gifted teacher and Zen master, this Vietnamese poet writes with loving insight about what Zen can mean in an individual's personal life. He is the author of many books, and the recommended reading is a compilation of some of his best. Another favorite is *The Miracle of Mindfulness*. Nominated for the Nobel Peace Prize by Martin Luther King Jr., Thich Nhat Hanh lives outside Paris where he writes and teaches as well as involving himself in the plight of refugees of all nations.

≺⸻

Ross, Nancy Wilson. *The World of Zen*.
New York: Random House, 1960.

Though written over thirty-five years ago, this anthology provides selected reading and poetry over the entire spectrum of Buddhism and

Zen. It is the kind of book the reader can skip around in. However, the early chapters give an excellent overview for the beginner.

🖎

Smith, Huston. *The Religions of Man.*
New York: Harper & Row, 1961.

Huston Smith is a giant in the study of comparative religions. His book *The Religions of Man* provides a clear and readable overview of the world's great religions. The section on Buddhism and Zen Buddhism provides an objective view of this often overly complicated subject. What is fascinating (if the reader will invest the time) is to review all the world's great metaphysical systems *and discover how similar they are!*

🖎

Suzuki, Shunryu. *Zen Mind, Beginner's Mind.*
New York: Weatherhill, 1983.

This early apostle of Zen, Shunryu Suzuki settled in the San Francisco area and rapidly created a total Zen Buddhist establishment, which grew into both Zen centers and a retreat monastery. This book is the first one recommended to beginners at these teaching and practice centers.

Index of First Lines